FaçadeGreenery

contemporary landscaping

The Deutsche Nationalbibliothek lists this publication in the Deutsche Nationalbibliografie; detailed bibliographical data are available on the internet at http://dnb.d-nb.de.

ISBN 978-3-03768-075-9
© 2011 by Braun Publishing AG
www.braun-publishing.ch

1st edition 2011

Project coordination: Editorial office van Uffelen
Editorial staff: Lisa Rogers, Chris van Uffelen
Translation preface: Geoffrey Steinherz
Graphic concept: Manuela Roth, Berlin
Layout: Natascha Saupe, Sara Dame

Chris van Uffelen

FaçadeGreenery

contemporary landscaping

BRAUN

Content

Preface

The Hanging Gardens of Semiramis are among the most legendary wonders of the antique world. The lack of written sources concerning the building, but also the fact that the association with Semiramis was first made in modern times, and the lack of historical context concerning this gardens makes it all the more mystical. Supposedly the terraces lay directly next to or inside the palace in Babylon. Nebuchadnezzar II is said to have built them for his wife Amyitis around 600 B.C. They are first described in the fourth century B.C. At 100 B.C. at the latest, the gardens must have perished along with the city. Today it has been established, that the term "hanging gardens" involves an error in translation from the Greek, and that planted roof terraces would be more correct. Especially in the desert landscape, these require a complicated irrigation system. However, the location of the gardens in the palace is a still a matter of dispute today. Even if most of the reconstructions correctly assume a terrace construction the puzzling term "hanging gardens" persists in the afterlife of the myth, in part merging with the equally mythical Tower of Babel.

The idea of a wall of green as more than just a protruding hedge, but rather something that emerges from the architecture itself, persisted. For centuries nature was transplanted into buildings with the use of climbing or hanging plants. Even today the terraced building is firmly associated with the idea of planting, with enough light and water to support a luxurious vegetation. But in the 21st century a new form of façade planting was created. In 2001 Patrick Blanc designed the first Vertical Garden in the context of the interior design of André Putman's Pershing Hall in Paris. Many tropical plants, grasses and perennials, which grow on trees, are planted up the face of the wall. What had previously been possible at lower heights, now flourished at the height of the building. In 2006 a change in the building code created Paris as a center for the new species, so that in that year, 39 vertical gardens were created. These require special irrigation systems with the relevant support mechanism attached to the outer wall like a cladding. A precise planting scheme is required, allowing an attractive façade to emerge. Up to 30 plants per square meter are required in order to form a dense green texture. The resulting green wall is a 90–100 degree transposition of the customary view of the landscape architect: a carpet transformed into a tapestry.

In addition to these modern vertical gardens this volume also contains "traditional hanging" and upwardly growing façade plants, which present the entire spectrum of the species of contemporary nature in architecture. More than its architectural-aesthetic aspects, the measures it can provide against the sealing of the soil surface, deforestation and a lack of urban recreation also make it a political and urban developmental topic. From the attempt to combine elements of nature with an urban construction density, a layer of green emerges, which settles over the city like a blanket. If one did not know that the plants had been artificially arranged and distributed on and infront of the wall, one could imagine that nature had begun to reclaim the city.

Friedrich Justin Bertuch: The floating (hanging) Gardens of Babylon, 1806 (Detail).

Pershing Hall Hotel

Paris, France
Landscape Design: Patrick Blanc
Interior Architecture: Andrée Putman
Completion: 2001
Client: Pershing Hall
Photos: Pershing Hall (8, 10), Chris van Uffelen (11)

This 30-meter-high vertical garden in the restaurant of the Pershing Hall Hotel in Paris was designed by Patrick Blanc, whose copyrighted 'murs végétaux' are revolutionizing urban gardens worldwide. Blanc's gardens are ingenious works of art, planted without soil on a durable frame of PVC, metal, and non-biodegradable felt, with a built-in pump watering system that allows them to thrive for years. This wall was designed using one centimeter thick PVC board and felt, the felt is stapled onto the PVC boards and plants are then inserted into the felt pockets, staples are then used to set the plants firmly. The individuality seen in all of Blanc's designs comes from the individually selected plants he uses.

Left: Inner courtyard with restaurant.
Right: Plan of the plant arrangement.

Top: Buffet in front of the vertical garden.
Bottom: Restaurant by night.
Right: Vertical garden.

M2 Metro Station

Lausanne, Switzerland
Architecture: Bernard Tschumi Architects with
M+V Merlini & Ventura Architectes
Completion: 2008
Client: TL Transit Lausanne, City of Lausanne
Photos: Peter Mauss/Esto, New York

As the main ticket office, this building needed to convey a public image for the transit authority and the city as a whole. The main gesture of the project is the folded concrete, which acts as though a strip of the plaza has been folded and bent back on itself to accommodate a ticket office to the east, and a pedestrian ramp to the subterranean level on the west. The rupture and folds are reminiscent of the topography of Lausanne and the geological history of the Alps. The roof and west wall are covered in a green carpet of plantings, which addresses environmental concerns of the client, but also incorporates a landscaped berm into a sunken oval, opening the subterranean light rail to natural daylight.

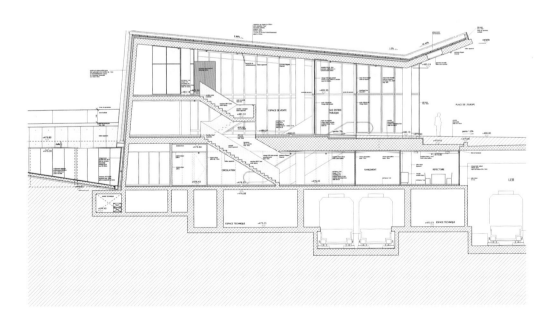

Left: East elevation, façade.
Right: Section.

Top: View of M2 and Interface FLON from the north.
Bottom: Bird's-eye view.
Right: View from the Place de l'Europe.

Ballet Valet Parking Garage

Miami Beach, FL, USA
Landscape Design: Rosenberg Gardner Design
Architecture: Arquitectonica
Completion: 1996
Client: Goldman Properties Company
Photos: Dan Forer (16, 18 b., 19), Dennis Wilhelm (18 a.)

The Ballet Valet Parking Garage is a six-level parking garage for 646 vehicles, located in the historic Art Deco District in South Beach. The upper garage façade is composed of grid patterned, fiberglass components, consisting of different levels that incorporate horizontal wave designs, reminiscent of the ocean. Within the grill-work, and spanning the entire length of each elevation on all levels, are planters with various types of vines and landscaping. The five stories of parking become a vertical green zone, a monumental sculpture completed in topiary. The street level of the structure is a band of historic Art Deco façades that were restored as part of the project.

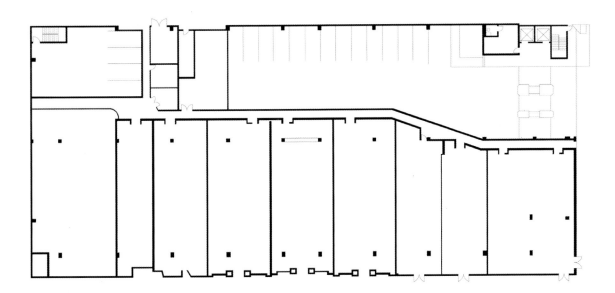

Left: East façade.
Right: Floor plan.

Top: Detail of trellises and vegetation. North-east corner.
Bottom: North elevation along Collins Avenue.
Right: South-west elevation at 7th Street and Collins Avenue.

House near Brussels

Brussels, Belgium
Landscape Design: Patrick Blanc
Architecture: Philippe Samyn and Partners
Completion: 2007
Client: Confidential
Photos: Marie Françoise Plissart

This house was built for an artist and includes the street level of an already existing house. The house includes curved walls of vegetation that are private and closed off from the neighbors to the north, east and south. In contrast, the west façade is composed entirely of a glass wall. Initially conceived as a wall of ivy with a copper roof, the vegetation of the façade was finally composed of a selection of exotic plants, chosen by the botanical artist Patrick Blanc, the vegetation expands to cover the roof. The insulation, waterproofing and irrigation were designed by architects Samyn and Partners. The plants are set into the walls with felt and supported by rigid PVC panels.

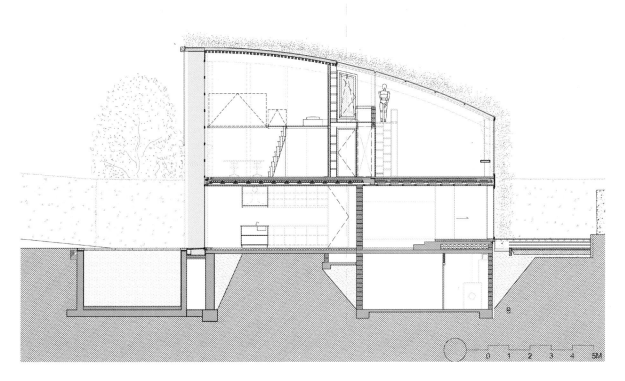

Left: The façade consists of greenery extending to the roof.
Right: Section.

Top: Interior view.
Bottom: Glass façade.
Right: Interior view.

22

Shinjuku Gardens

Tokyo, Japan
Landscape Design: cheungvogl
Architecture: cheungvogl
Completion: 2012
Client: Confidential
Photos: cheungvogl/TOYOit, Hong Kong

Land is scarce in the inner city of Tokyo and restful green spaces are few and far between. 'Shinjuku Gardens' – in the thriving hub of Tokyo's inner city, is a conscious effort to make the most of the available open space; pushing boundaries in a quest to amalgamate much needed natural landscape into the infrastructure of the city. The project raises economical, social, environmental and cultural awareness of various aspects. The design strategies aim to maximize investment returns by providing more than double the amount of car parking spaces; optimize opportunities to inject greenscape to reduce CO_2 exhaust emissions, and promote arts and culture by offering space for art exhibitions in the city center of Tokyo.

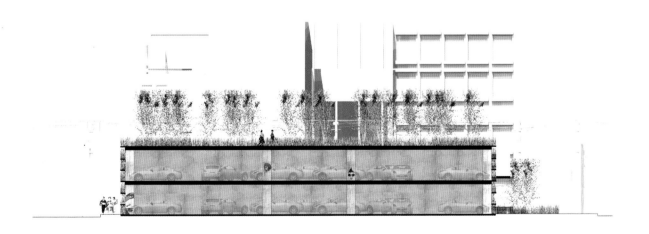

Left: Perspective, street level.
Right: Section.

Top: Façade. Parking level.
Bottom: Perspective, interior.
Right: Street elevation.

Consorcio - Santiago Building

Santiago, Chile
Architecture: Enrique Browne and Borja Huidobro
Completion: 1993
Client: Consorcio Nacional de Seguros
Photos: Enrique Browne (28, 30 r. a.), Guy Wenborne
(30 l. a.), Cristian Barahona (30 b.), Jaime Villaseca (31)

This project involves two long volumes that create a gallery, providing access to the building. The treatment of the façades deserves special attention. A western façade in Santiago produces serious heating problems during the summer. Therefore, the building was improved with technical and natural resources, producing a double façade consisting of an inner with curtain wall and an outer with vegetation. This 'double vegetal façade' reduces solar absorption. In addition it transforms the building into a vertical garden. The vegetation enlivens the building, giving it a cheerful look that changes appearance with the seasons.

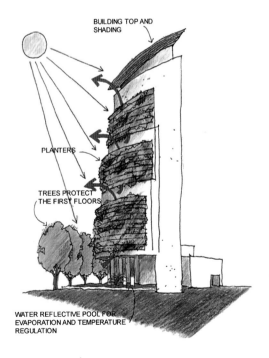

Left: Street elevation.
Right: Thermic functioning sketch.

Top: Meeting room. Double vegetal skin in summer.
Bottom: Night elevation.
Right: Detail, double vegetal skin.

House Reid

Salt Rock, Kwazulu Natal, South Africa
Landscape Design: Leon Kluge
Architecture: Dean Jay of Jay and Nel Arch
Completion: 2010
Client: Fiona and Diederick Reid
Photos: Sven Musica, Nelspruit, RSA

This garden is part of the external wall directly next to the lap pool. The main living areas face both the vertical garden on the northern side of the house and the Indian Ocean on the eastern side. The boundary wall is extremely high and would have had a very negative impact on the aesthetics of the house if left bare. The garden not only had to soften this wall and bring greenery to an area where there would have been none but also had to fit in with the ultra modern design of the house. Brightly colored plants were used to put the emphasis on the garden and not on the wall. Some of the plants used are, Bromeliads, ferns, Ophiopogon, Sedum and Alternathera. The brief was that the garden had to hang like a tapestry.

Left: Frontal detail.
Right: Perspective of the plant arrangement.

33

Top: Living wall with view to the ocean.
Bottom: Pool area.
Right: Angled detail.

El Japonez

Mexico City, Mexico
Landscape Design: Guillermo Arredondo
Architecture: Cheremserrano
Completion: 2007
Client: Gastronomica Nigiri
Photos: Jaime Navarro, Spain

A large open space, full of light, with virtually no columns, covered in wood and plants: this design concept becomes reality in this restaurant. Vegetation is incorporated in an original way, not by using weak elements such as flowerpots, but through the incorporation of a long living wall. The floor of the restaurant is covered by a plastic carpet that evokes the tatami of Japanese architecture. The scarcity of columns is evident: only one column is clearly present, which creates the impression that this long stretch is supported by only one structural element. The rest of the columns have been hidden so as to avoid interrupting the flow of light and space.

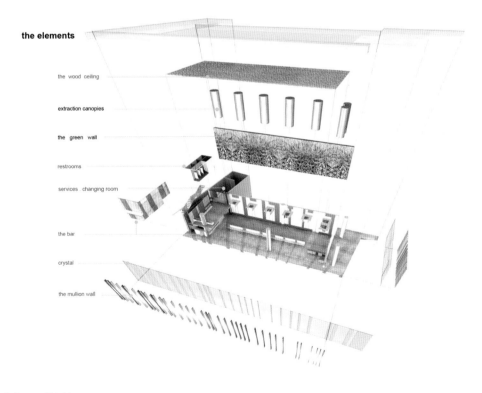

the elements

the wood ceiling

extraction canopies

the green wall

restrooms

services . changing room

the bar

crystal

the mullion wall

Left: Green wall, Tepanyaki tables.
Right: Structural diagram.

Top: Tepanyaki tables and bar.
Bottom: Perspective.
Right: View through the restaurant.

Acros Fukuoka

Fukuoka, Japan
Architecture: Emilio Ambasz & Associates, Inc.
Completion: 1995
Client: Dai-ichi Mutual Life Insurance Co.
Photos: Hiromi Watanabe

Among Emilio Ambasz' recent projects, Acros Fukuoka is the most power-ful synthesis of urban and park forms. Its north face presents an elegant urban façade with a formal entrance, appropriate to a building on the most prestigious street in Fukuoka's financial district. A series of terraced gardens that climb the full height of the building, extend along the south side of the hall, culminating in a magnificent belvedere that offers a breathtaking view of the city's harbor. Below the park's 15, one-story terraces lies over 100,000 square meters of multipurpose space containing an exhibition hall, a museum, theater, and government offices.

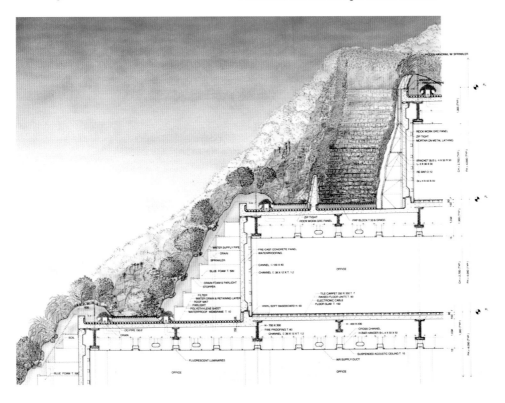

Left: Exterior elevation, skylight.
Right: Section.

Top: Interior view. Detail of the façade.
Bottom: Exterior elevation.
Right: Bird's-eye view.

MFO-Park Zurich

Zurich, Switzerland
Architecture: planergemeinschaft MFO-Park
burckhardtpartner / raderschallpartner ag
Structural Engineering: Basler & Hofmann
Completion: 2002
Client: Grün Stadt Zürich
Photos: raderschallpartner ag

The second of four parks planned for the new Zurich North center, with roughly 5,000 residents and 12,000 workplaces, is comprised of a hall, filled and covered with plants. More than 100-meters long and 17-meters high, the steel structure forms a three-dimensional 'urban arbour'. In between the inner and outer-planted skins is a route consisting of steel stairs and walkways, with wood-paved loggias cantilevered out internally. The peaceful garden spaces are ideal for relaxation, but can also be used for stage performances and concerts. A pool of water and seating facilities are set within an area of green glass chippings. Here, stainless-steel cables extend up to the roof as trellises for climbing plants.

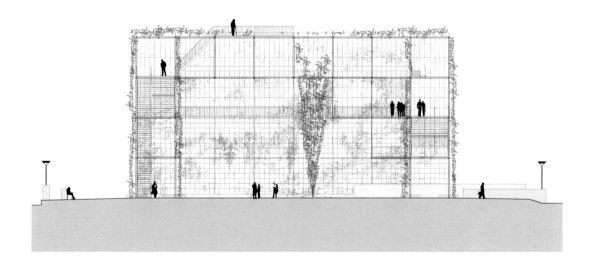

Left: View from the upper floor.
Right: Cross section.

Top: Façade and entrances. View from above.
Bottom: Street elevation.
Right: Greenery detail.

Calzada de los Sabinos

San Pedro Garza García, Mexico
Landscape Design: Ecotono Urbano
Architecture: Biozotea
Completion: 2009
Client: Private
Photos: Oswaldo Zurita Zaragoza, Monterrey

This green wall is the largest one ever designed for a private residence in Mexico. It was designed to integrate the house into its lush surroundings; the living wall has now become a microhabitat for wildlife and provides an amazing view from almost any room in the house. The lines that define the design of the green wall compliment the design principles used for the furniture inside the house, where there are almost no parallel or curved lines. The exuberant and dense green wall provokes a spectacular contrast with the architectural simplicity of the house, making the plants on the wall the main visual attraction. Only local materials and plants grown in the area were used in this project.

Left: Ferns stand out one meter away from the wall base.
Right: Masterplan of the living wall.

49

Top: Aspect of the living wall and the background mountains during winter.
Bottom: Vegetation growing wild.
Right: Vertical garden contrasts with simple horizontal garden.

Natura Towers

Lisbon, Portugal
Landscape Design: Vertical Garden Design
Architecture: GJP
Completion: 2009
Client: MSF
Photos: Michael Hellgren

This project consists of an indoor garden in the entrance area and an outdoor garden around a public square between two buildings. The outdoor wall wraps around three sides of the square, facing south, east and north. The north facing wall enjoys a protected location with no direct sunlight at all. It hosts a variety of ferns and many broad leaved plant species. Together, these different areas create a moist, woodland feel. The east facing wall has very little direct sunlight. Plants with similar character as on the north wall have been chosen. The south facing wall is shadowed by one of the buildings, but still, the sun exposure creates significantly different growing conditions. Unlike the other walls, this wall hosts flowering plants and is more colorful.

Left: Stairs along east facing wall.
Right: Plan of the plants arrangement.

Top: Indoor wall with main entrance in the background. North facing wall.
Bottom: From left to right: north, east and south facing wall.
Right: Indoor wall separated by a small water fall.

Edipresse

Lausanne, Switzerland
Landscape Design: Hüsler & Associés architectes paysagistes
Architecture: Hüsler & Associés architectes paysagistes
Completion: 2009
Client: Edipresse SA, Lausanne
Photos: Courtesy of the architects

The existing Edipresse building in Lausanne was extended with a four-story annex. Two green bands, 7x0.8 meters, were intergrated into the north façade, positioned so that they are visible from the offices. These have the effect of breaking up the large, plain façade. To provide a contrast to the shadowy appearance of this side of the building, plants with a light green leaf were used. A carpet of perennial plants was utilized, combined with Hosta and Japanese ornamental maple. This unusual combination has the added advantage of surprising observers throughout the year as it changes in color and appearance.

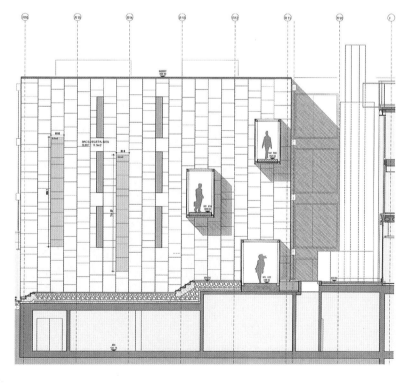

Left: Worm's-eye view.
Right: Plan façade.

Top: Side elevation.
Bottom: Elevation.
Right: Detail, façade.

Theater foyer

Groningen, The Netherlands
Landscape Design: Sempergreen Vertical Systems BV
Architecture: Sempergreen Vertical Systems BV
Completion: 2010
Client: Grand Theater Groningen
Photos: Sempergreen Vertical Systems BV

This indoor green wall is located in the foyer of a theater, behind a bar. The wall is designed to give the impression that the plants are naturally growing behind the wall. The focus of this façade is on attention to detail, the panels were grown before they were installed and feature a variety of plants. Species of plants with a large leaf were chosen to give the wall a lush, green appearance. The depth of the greenery creates a pleasant atmosphere for visitors entering the foyer area. It is also an unusual feature, bringing the outdoors indoors, providing a meeting place and talking point at the same time as offering visual variety.

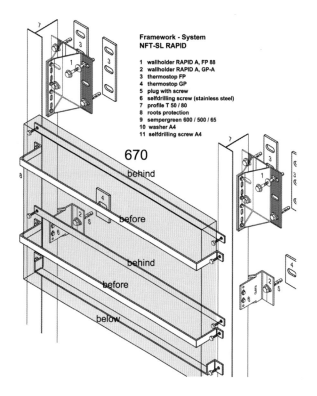

Framework - System
NFT-SL RAPID

1 wallholder RAPID A, FP 88
2 wallholder RAPID A, GP-A
3 thermostop FP
4 thermostop GP
5 plug with screw
6 selfdrilling screw (stainless steel)
7 profile T 50 / 80
8 roots protection
9 sempergreen 600 / 500 / 65
10 washer A4
11 selfdrilling screw A4

Left: Vertical garden behind the bar.
Right: Framework.

Top: Vertical garden behind the bar.
Bottom: Perspective.
Right: Detail living wall.

Ex Ducati

Rimini, Italy
Architecture: Mario Cucinella Architects
Façade: Facadesign snc
Completion: 2008
Client: Edile Carpentieri
Photos: Daniele Domenicali

This building has an 'L' shaped layout, facing onto a major road junction. The façades describe a 90-degree arc and are clad with a planted, green skin, creating a compact urban frontage. The green skin is made from a steel grid where climbing plants are encouraged to grow, creating an uninterrupted screen over the entire length of the building. The rear façade of the building is finished with wooden, cladding elements. The envelope is formed from a stainless steel grid, secured to the structure of cantilevered galleries that provide access to the offices. The steel grid forms a supporting structure for climbing plants, creating the appearance of vertical hanging gardens, reminiscent of ivy covered buildings.

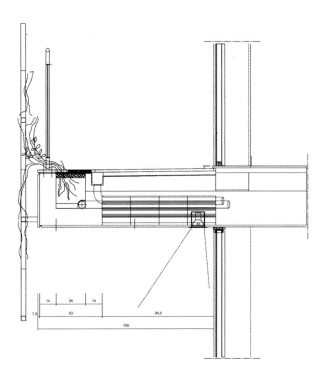

Left: Entrance area.
Right: Façade, planting detail.

Top: Walkways and climbing plants. South-west façade.
Bottom: Street elevation.
Right: Façade, detail.

Open house TEC

San Pedro Garza García, Mexico
Landscape Design: Ecotono Urbano
Architecture: Biozotea
Completion: 2010
Client: Sorteo TEC
Photos: Oswaldo Zurita Zaragoza, Monterrey

This design was completed by Biozotea for Open House Tec in Mexico. Vertical gardens are not very common in Monterrey and this is one of the first in the area. By installing this wall in a place where it can be seen by members of the public, visitors can see that living in a small space does not mean that nature has to stay outside. The green wall includes a significant diversity of plants, using more than 20 species in only 15 square meters and includes plants that can grow and develop in shaded areas. The biopared works very well as an artistic background for an art piece.

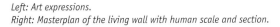

Left: Art expressions.
Right: Masterplan of the living wall with human scale and section.

Top: View from the bar. Diversity of plants.
Bottom: View from the main entrance to the house.
Right: A wild and diverse living wall.

Pioneer Headquarters

Paine, Chile
Architecture: Enrique Browne with Tomás Swett
Completion: 2009
Client: Pioneer Chile
Photos: Guy Wenborne (72), Felipe Fontecilla (74 a., 75),
Enrique Brown (74 b.)

This project, by Enrique browne and Tomás Swett, involved the regeneration and improvement of the Pioneer Headquarters in Chile. A park, extending the whole length of the site's front was established, improving the public aspect of the factory. Previous construction projects at the factory had generated large accumulations of soil. These were used to form slopes with grass and trees that reach along the walls and sloping roof of the building, blending the offices with the park and isolating them from noise. The entrance to the premises is through a groove in the northern boundary. The private offices and meeting rooms open onto the central gardens that continue the park, generating natural ventilation.

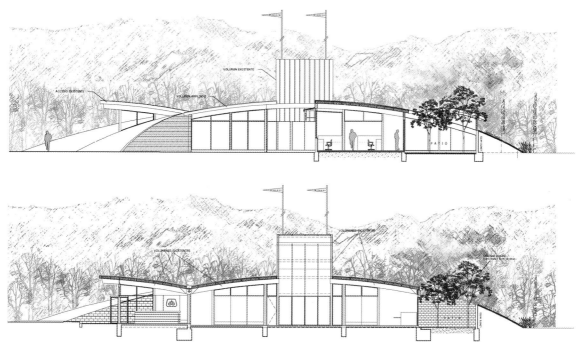

Left: Aerial view showing African grasses and aloes.
Right: Sections.

Top: Lateral view Pioneer extension building.
Bottom: Exterior elevation.
Right: Interior view.

home 06

Amsterdam, The Netherlands
Landscape Design: Green Fortune
Architecture: i29 interior architects
Completion: 2010
Client: Confidential
Photos: Courtesy of the architects

This residence in Amsterdam is all about clever usage of the small space available. Integration of nature is an important aspect of traditional culture in Japan, the homeland of the client. The integrated in-house vertical garden is an example of this. The bathroom and bedroom are hidden in a volume, placed at the back of the house. From the open living area you look towards the vertical garden and the entrance stairs to the roof terrace, the garden offers a feeling of seclusion and secrecy and the panorama created by the vertical garden and the contrast of this feature with the minimalist, white bed / bathroom provides an intense experience.

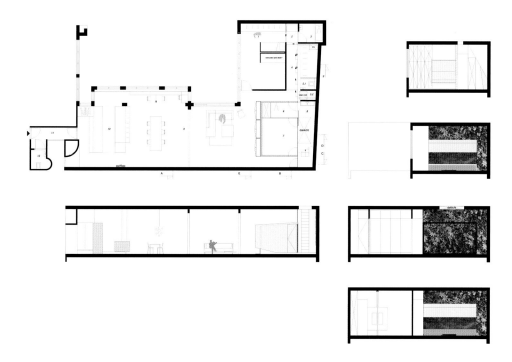

Left: Perspective, bathroom and stairs.
Right: Building plans with living wall.

Top: Interior view.
Bottom: Bathroom and stairs to the roof terrace.
Right: Perspective bathroom.

Serre des jardins

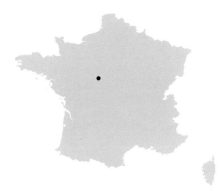

Chaumont-sur-Loire, France
Architecture: Edouard François, Duncan Lewis
Completion: 1999
Client: Festival der Jardins á Chaumont-sur-Loire
Photos: Blaise Porte

Created in the context of a prominent international garden festival, this greenhouse takes 'anti-design' and 'low-tech' as the basis of its attempt to celebrate the architecture of the ordinary by experimenting with a whole range of materials and techniques. The ultra-light structure weighs only one ton and covers an area of 150 square meters. Bamboo pilers carrying the PVC cover are interconnected by practically invisible twine. Eyelets reinforced with rubber gaskets accommodate guy-wires which anchor the structure externally. Air enters the greenhouse via 30 ventilators embedded in the cover. The bamboo structure is echoed by the vegetation carpeting of the greenhouse's surroundings and this continuity fosters the fusion of the exterior and interior.

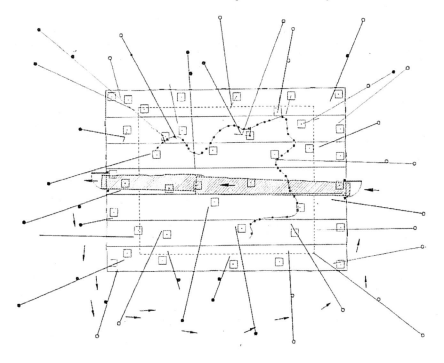

Left: Entrance.
Right: Sketch.

Top: Twilight. Impression.
Bottom: View at night.
Right: Bamboo piles.

Sihlcity

Zurich, Switzerland
Landscape Design: raderschallpartner ag landschafts-architekten
Architecture: Theo Hotz AG, Kuhn Fischer Partner Architekten AG, Vehovar + Jauslin Architektur
Completion: 2007
Client: Credit Suisse, Swiss Prime Site AG
Photos: raderschallpartner ag

This project is defined by its innovative use of vegetation within a densely populated area, bringing greenery to the urban space. The large, open surface areas are brought to life by carefully designed areas of vegetation and water features. The artificial landscape brings the city closer to nature, opening the space out. Closely set willow trees in the neighboring square give the area a special quality. The neighboring square, Kalandarplatz, provides a space for events throughout the year, the green façade, seating and willow trees give the area a garden atmosphere.

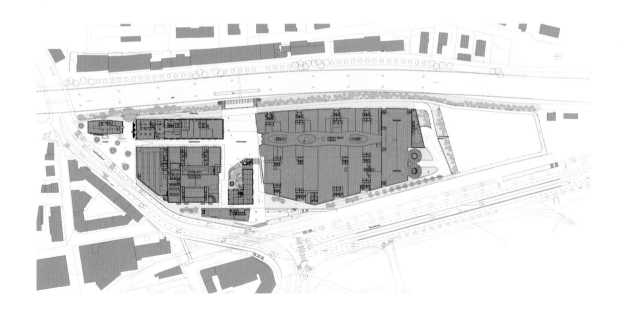

Left: Green façade, parking area.
Right: Site plan.

Top: Steps covered with greenery.
Bottom: Detail, façade. Façade.
Right: Perspective.

DIGI Technology Operation Center

Shah Alam, Selangor, Malaysia
Landscape Design: T. R. Hamzah & Yeang Sdn. Bhd.
Architecture: T. R. Hamzah & Yeang Sdn. Bhd.
Completion: 2010
Client: DIGI Telecommunications Sdn. Bhd.
Photos: Robert Such

This project was designed for a data center, with the aim was of providing effective drainage and waterproofing to protect sensitive equipment as well as reducing solar heat gain inside the data center. The façades incorporate extensive, vertical green walls that act as living habitats. The large greenery component also acts as a means of filtering and improving the indoor air quality. The green wall reduces solar gain, therefore reducing energy costs, as well as trapping dust, reducing noise and providing a habitat for urban wildlife. Collected rainwater is used to irrigate the plant system, reducing water waste and improving the center's carbon footprint.

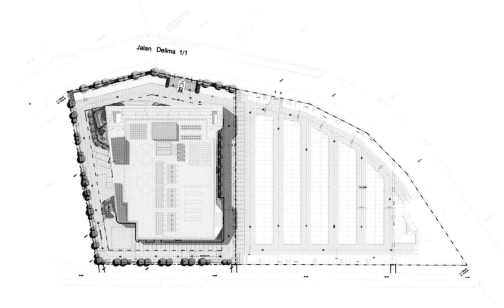

Left: Street elevation.
Right: Ground floor plan.

Top: Elevation. Detail, façade.
Bottom: Detail.
Right: Overview.

Replay Florence

Florence, Italy
Landscape Design: Vertical Garden Design
Architecture: Studio 10
Completion: 2009
Client: Replay
Photos: Michael Hellgren

This project at the new Replay concept store in Florence was completed in spring 2009. The vertical garden is part of an ecological theme, developed by the architects. It covers a seven-meter-high L-shaped wall in the three-story boutique. The garden is inspired by the undergrowth of a temperate forest, the overall picture is a soft yet dense. The somewhat dark greenery includes some small-flowering plants like lanterns on top of the darker background. There is a base of plants with medium sized leaves and various ferns. Within this framework, there are solitary species with stronger characters some that are flowering, others with special colored or textured leaves. Size and growth habit were important criteria when choosing the plants.

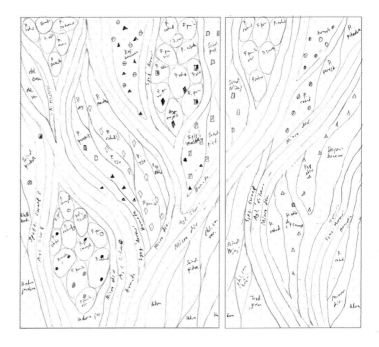

Left: View from outside.
Right: Sketch of the plant arrangement.

Top: View to vertical garden from second floor. Interior view.
Bottom: Interior view, first floor.
Right: Detail, plants and jeans.

Spidernethewood

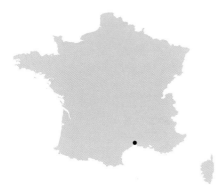

Nîmes, France
Landscape Design: R&Sie(n)-Paris
Architecture: R&Sie(n)-Paris
Completion: 2007
Client: Urbain and Elisabeth Souriau
Photos: Courtesy of the architects

A dwelling like a spiderweb in the middle of the forest: To create this extraordinary project, big, mesh spiderweb was constructed in an existing forest. A plastic mesh nets and wraps around the trees to produce a labyrinth in the branches. It includes a 450 square meter indoor building on two floors, plugged into this labyrinth by a huge, sliding glass door. The boundaries between inside and outside become a blur. Within five years, the Spidernethewood will be lost in the surroundings, by then the plastic mesh will be integrated into the forest, the web-house will be all parabolic arcs and delirious sagging.

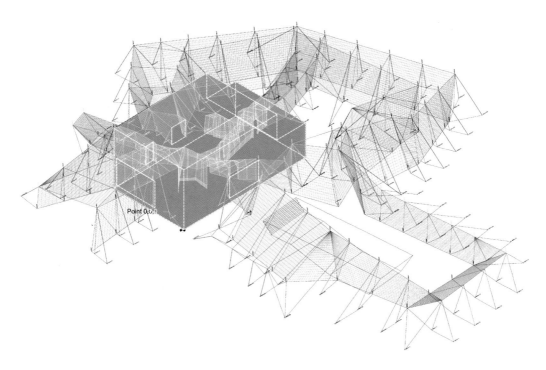

Left: Path to the entrance.
Right: Labyrinth of nets.

Top: Path through the fences.
Bottom: Swimming pool area.
Right: Interior view to the outside.

Theater Studio for University

Brno, Czech Republic
Landscape Design: Archteam
Architecture: Archteam with RadaArchitecti
Completion: 2011
Client: Academy of Arts Brno
Renderings: Archteam

The Theater Studio for University JAMŪ is situated in the historical center of the city of Brno. The house itself is constructed of concrete and composed of two main areas; the theater house itself is leveled with the street, surrounded by older houses. The second area is a large garden, the green façade connects the house visually to the large garden area. Small windows can be seen peering out through the greenery, their size allows light into the building but does not disrupt the continuation of the green façade. At the front of the theater, large, glass windows allow light into the building and give it an approachable feeling, welcoming passers-by in from the street.

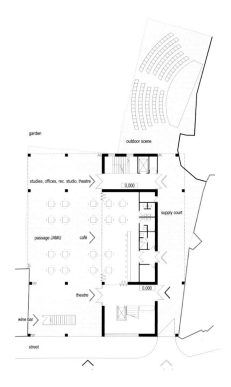

Left: View from the Minorit´s garden.
Right: Ground floor plan.

Top: Bird's-eye view. Perspective.
Bottom: View from Orli street.
Right: Perspective.

Musée du Quai Branly

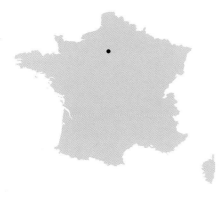

Paris, France
Landscape Design: Patrick Blanc (vegetal wall)
Architecture: Atelier Jean Nouvel
Completion: 2006
Client: Etablissement public du Musée du Quai Branly
Photos: Patric Blanc (106), Chris van Uffelen (104, 107)

This museum collects various exhibits stemming from non-European cultures which were earlier dispersed among the city's various museums. The building is located in a generous garden, and the ground story remains open, allowing the garden sections to fuse underneath the museum. The 18,000 square-meter garden takes up diverse vegetation as its theme. A 12-meter-high, 200-meter-long glass wall shields the park from the busy Quai Branly. The 800 square meters of the exterior and 150 square meters of the interior of the green wall along the west perimeter along Quai Branly bring together 15,000 examples of plants from Japan, China, the Americas and Central Europe.

Left: Vegetal wall covering the façade of the Branly administrative building.
Right: Section.

Top: Street elevation.
Bottom: Vegetal wall.
Right: Detail, façade.

Biopark

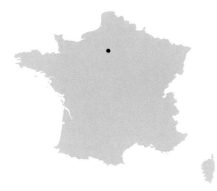

Paris, France
Landscape Design: Raphia
Architecture: Valode et Pistre
Completion: 2006
Client: Sagi
Photos: Michel Denancé

The structure of this imposing building, a witness of its time, remains unchanged. The intervention reframes, restructures and redefines the form. The constructed volumes are split, transforming the heart of the urban block into squares. The cut gable ends are dressed in a metal trellis, creating a support for vegetation. Formerly austere, the heart of the block becomes a green environment with façades stepped into terraces, doubled by a generous wave-like pergola on which roses, bellflowers, acanthuses and clematises grow. The courses are held behind this vegetable cascade, which protects the offices from the sun and floods the area with its presence.

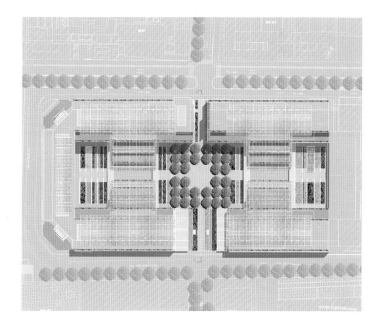

Left: Street elevation.
Right: Site plan.

Top: Inner courtyard.
Bottom: Rear elevation.
Right: Street elevation.

Casino Hollywood

Monterrey, Mexico
Landscape Design: Ecotono Urbano
Architecture: Biozotea
Completion: 2007
Client: Hollywood Casino
Photos: Oswaldo Zurita Zaragoza, Monterrey

Green roofs and living walls are still incipient elements of the urban landscape in Monterrey, Mexico, a city of extreme temperatures. This project is one of the first examples of vertical gardens with public access in the city. It was first conceived only as an aesthetic solution to improve the façade facing the most important avenue in the city, but during the design the firm proposed to use condensate water from the air conditioning system to irrigate the biopared, this strategy allows not only the living wall to use this sustainable source water, but all gardens around the building, saving more the 75,700 liter per year and the rosemary planted on the biopared is being used to decorate the daily buffet, offered by the casino.

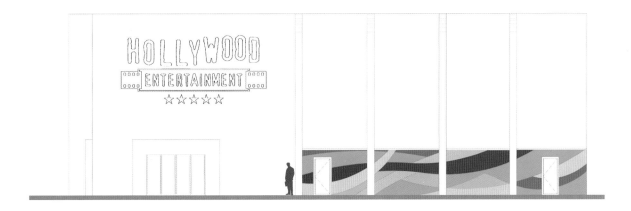

Left: Volume and texture are important elements of this living wall.
Right: Masterplan of the living wall with human scale.

Top: The green wall facing the street.
Bottom: After two months from installation.
Right: One of the four sections of the green wall.

House F

Alicante, Spain
Architecture: Joaquin Alvado
Completion: 2007
Client: Confidential
Photos: Courtesy of the architects

The ground floor occupies the total area of the available space, which is about 700 square meters. Interior and exterior exist in an uncertain relation to each other. The programs of the housing lower to the ground floor level, whereas the garden extends to the top floors. The building becomes an inhabitable landscape and a dynamic structure. The reflections of the glass are arranged in the diverse planes of House F and incorporate the vegetation and the sky in the elevations.

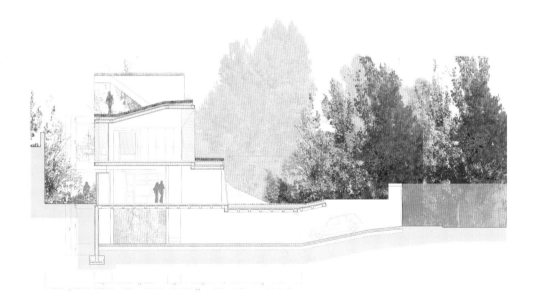

Left: Rear elevation.
Right: Section.

Top: Street elevation.
Bottom: Garden view.
Right: Backyard with swimming pool.

Hilltop Estate

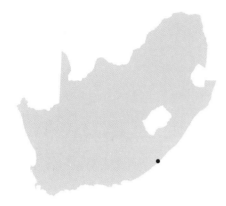

Ballito, South Africa
Landscape Design: Uys & White Landscape Architects
Completion: 2007
Client: Elides Investments cc
Photos: Lucas Uys

Hilltop was planned as a residential estate with approximately 100 sites. The entrance is positioned in the steep topography. The required retaining wall, with a height of six meters, had to be softened to accommodate the environmental requirements of the estate. Thus, the wall was punctuated with apertures planted with rock figs, creating dynamic root sculptures on the rough textured wall, which was colored using local soil pigments. The understated gate house is covered by a flat roof, greened with African grasses and aloes. The estate's landscape forms part of the sensitive KwaZulu Natal Coastal Forest Eco-System.

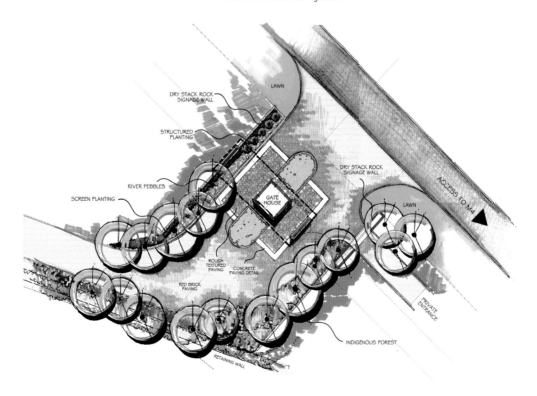

Left: Aerial view showing African grasses and aloes.
Right: Plan of plant arrangement.

Top: Rock fig in pre-cast planter. Gate house with African landscape.
Bottom: Gate house with Rock fig wall in backdrop.
Right: Rhythm of Rock figs.

House Wilson

Grabouw, Western Cape, South Africa
Landscape Design: Leon Kluge
Architecture: Alan Walt Architect + Associates
Completion: 2010
Client: Wilson family
Photos: David Davidson

This garden is situated approximately 40 kilometers from Cape Town on a wine farm near Grabouw. Surrounded by beautiful mountains, vineyards and natural fynbos, the boutique hotel is designed on a strong axis, with the front door being the focal point of this axis. In order to emphasize the entrance it was decided that a vertical garden should be used. The garden faces west, which means that the plants are exposed to very harsh sun. Plants had to be chosen that would be able to withstand harsh conditions. Because of this, the designer used plants indigenous to the area: A lot of carnivorous plant were used of the Drosera species as well as Yuncus, Acorus, Kniphofia and Crassula.

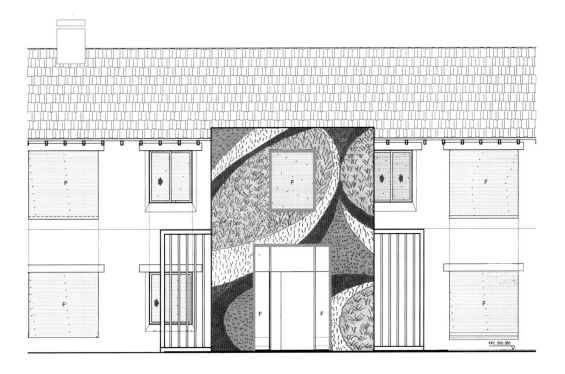

FFL 260.360

Left: Entrance.
Right: Plan of plant arrangement.

Top: Front elevation
Bottom: Door casing.
Right: Detail plants.

Procore

Nieuw-Vennep, The Netherlands
Landscape Design: Sempergreen Vertical Systems BV
Architecture: Sempergreen Vertical Systems BV
Completion: 2010
Client: Procore
Photos: Sempergreen Vertical Systems BV

The entrance to this office building in Holland was completely transformed after the installation of this Green Wall. The common brick wall turned into a lively, colorful and interesting green façade, designed to complement the building location, in a green neighborhood surrounded by canals. The green wall is of a south-west orientation and was planted with a mix of species to give it a wild appearance. The appearance of the wall alters with the seasons, providing habitat for birds and insects as well as bringing a sense of the outdoors to the users of the building. The irrigation is completely automatic and it is controlled by sensors, precisely delivering the exact amount of water and nutrients necessary, avoiding any waste.

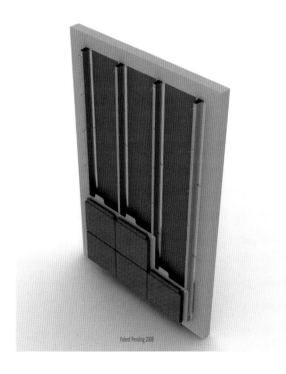

Left: Greened façade.
Right: Panel system.

Top: Wall with Buxus in front. Detail, plants in a black frame.
Bottom: Worm's-eye view.
Right: Detail plants.

Salad Bar

Cronulla, NSW, Australia
Landscape Design: Co-ordinated Landscapes and Elmich Australia
Architecture: Turf Design Studio
Completion: 2004
Client: Turf Design Studio
Photos: Simon Wood

The Salad Bar was featured at the 2004 Built Environment Future Gardens exhibition in the Royal Botanic Gardens in Sydney. The exhibition demonstrated how environmental sustainability could be practically incorporated into contemporary living. In 2005, the Salad Bar was invited to join the Houses of the Future exhibition held at Sydney Olympic Park. The project provides a modular, vertical growing structure with a footprint that is smaller than the generic garden, enabling it to occupy small spaces. Integrating a bar within the vegetated wall provides a playful vision of how self sufficiency can be incorporated into contemporary urban living.

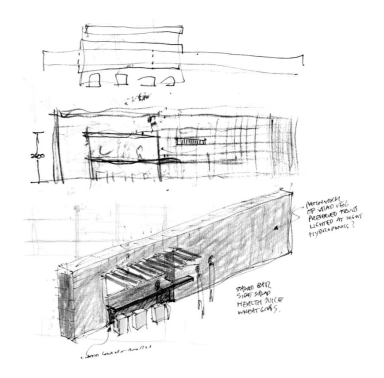

Left: Vertical gardens, the sky is the limit.
Right: Sketch.

Top: Detail of the wall. Children in front of the fresh salad.
Bottom: Bar detail.
Right: Salad bar at night.

Square Vinet

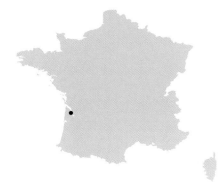

Bordeaux, France
Landscape Design: Patrick Blanc with Michael Desvigne
Completion: 2007
Photos: Patrick Blanc

Square Vinet is a contemporary square in Bordeaux in France. Its main feature is a 100-meter-long vertical garden, designed by French botanist, Patrick Blanc. This square offers a green space in the heart of the city. The vertical garden was constructed in 2007 and the design includes multiple plant species, textures and colors. The plants are positioned and held onto the wall surface with one-cm-thick PVC board and felt, the felt is stapled onto the PVC boards and plants are then inserted into the felt pockets, staples are then used to set the plants firmly. A fence protects the garden and the square is closed at night to avoid any damage being caused to the garden.

Left: Detail of the 100-meter-long vertical garden.
Right: Sketch.

Top: Green space in the city.
Bottom: People in front of the vertical garden.
Right: Detail.

Z58

Shanghai, China
Architecture: Kengo Kuma & Associates
Completion: 2006
Client: Zhongtai Lighting
Photos: Mitsumasa Fujitsuka

This building was designed by Kengo Kuma & Associates and is composed of a collection of interfaces. Suites and a garden are located at the top of the building to provide lodging and living space for designers that come from cities around the world to Shanghai to attend meetings. The lower portion of the building consists of an atrium, exhibition space and conference space that is surrounded by a 'glass waterfall', providing a gentle connection with Fanyu Road in front of the building. The façade has been created from 'green louvers', which are created with mirror finish stainless steel planter boxes to provide an evergreen vine cover that separates the atrium from Fanyu Road.

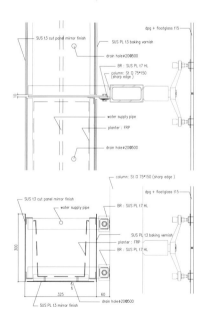

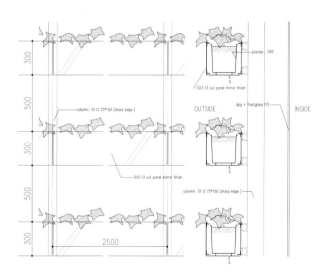

Left: Entrance area.
Right: Plan, detail façade.

Top: Detail façade. Interior view.
Bottom: Street elevation.
Right: Façade by night.

Solar das acacias

Maputo, Mozambique
Landscape Design: Leon Kluge
Architecture: CNBV
Completion: 2009
Client: Mr. and Mrs. Loureiro
Photos: Sven Musica, Nelspruit, RSA

This garden is situated on the main road of Maputo, Mozambique. The building has a beautiful mosaic artwork on the right hand side of the entrance. The garden would be the 'artwork' on the left side of the entrance, balancing the façade. The mosaic artwork was designed long before the garden and the green façade had to fit in with the theme. The building is very close to the beach and organic shapes were used in conjunction with circles to mimic the flow of water ending in a 'sun' shaped circle surrounding the top right window. This shape balances the mosaic sun on the other side of the entrance. Plants such as Bromeliads, orchids, ferns, Alternathera and Hemigraphis were used in this design.

Left: Street elevation.
Right: Plan of plant arrangement.

Top: Front elevation.
Bottom: Detail, façade.
Right: Detail, planting.

Academisch Ziekenhuis

Brussels, Belgium
Landscape Design: Philippe Samyn and Partners
Architecture: Philippe Samyn and Partners
Completion: 2007
Client: Academisch Ziekenhuis – Vrije Universiteit Brussels
Photos: Marie-Françoise Plissarts

This building was constructed to house the university hospital buildings and management offices in Brussels. The laboratory buildings are structured like a mound, so as not to disrupt the view from the surrounding buildings. The façades are covered with a coat of peat and ivy, this allows the building to blend into the site without hiding or overwhelming the existing buildings. The hospital's view of Brussels is thus maintained and the façade, covered in greenery, is also more attractive than a traditional flat roof. A number of high apertures let daylight penetrate deep into the laboratories. The offices on the upper floor have long horizontal bays with panoramic views and a broad terrace runs along the windows.

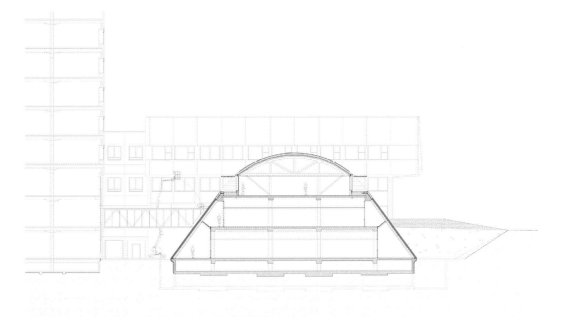

Left: Façade by night.
Right: Section.

Top: Interior view, offices. Interior view, cafeteria.
Bottom: Exterior elevation.
Right: Perspective, exterior.

Chan Center for the Performing Arts

Vancouver, Canada
Landscape Design: Cornelia Oberlander and Elizabeth Watts
Architecture: Bing Thom Architects
Completion: 1997
Client: University of British Columbia
Photos: Nic Lehoux

The Chan Center, designed by Bing Thom Architects, is located in the middle of a small forest of beautiful cedars and firs. The building is clad in natural materials that complement the building's verdant surrounding. The main form is clad in zinc panels that weather and evolve in appearance over time. During most of the year, ivy trails over the top and down the sides of the building, further concealing it within the setting and reflecting the changing seasons. BTA kept in mind that when designing a concert hall, what is actually being designed is a reverberation chamber. Thus, the charge for the architects was to design, essentially, the inside of a violin, to achieve the finest sound possible for concerts, music, and drama performances.

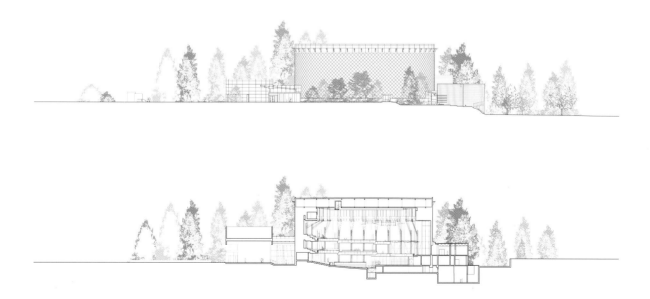

Left: Main entrance with greened façade.
Right: South façade and section.

Top: Entance. Interior concert hall.
Bottom: Garden.
Right: Foyer with reflections of green.

118 Elysées

Paris, France
Landscape Design: AW²
Architecture: AW²
Completion: 2006
Photos: Tendance Floue, Paris

AW² was appointed to carry out the complete refurbishment of an existing office building on the Avenue des Champs Elysées in Paris. The existing façades were completely refurbished, as well as all the interiors. The courtyard has been modified by introducing a vertical garden, which, in the contrived space changes both the look and feel of the whole building. This is the strongest feature, contributing to a renewed quality of workspace for all users. The entrance hall was also totally redesigned by introducing a white corian wall, decorated with a back-lit vegetal pattern, recalling the vertical garden of the central courtyard.

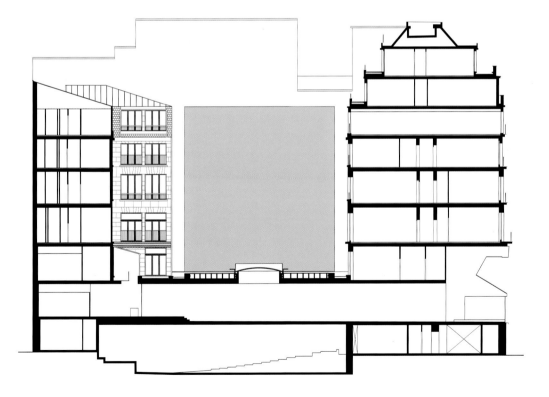

Left: The court with vertical garden.
Right: Section.

Top: Main entrance. Offices.
Bottom: Offices and the view of the vertical garden.
Right: Court with vertical garden.

Seed Posts

New York, NY, USA
Landscape Design and Artwork: Michele Brody
Completion: 2008
Client: AIG
Photos: Michele Brody, New York

This project looks to its historical form as hills of wild meadows, by adding a refreshing approach to ameliorating the daily life of city pedestrians. Lace-covered vertical planters temporarily attached to construction scaffolding provide a cool and refreshing environment amidst the steel and concrete. The premise behind the design of Seed Posts is to combine the space saving eco-technology of hydroponic vertical gardening with a domestic connection. This is created by incorporating the use of lace curtain fabric with annual grasses amongst the public construction environment of the city streets. The outer surface serves as an aesthetic choice, referencing the 'quaintness' of the home interior within the open city streets.

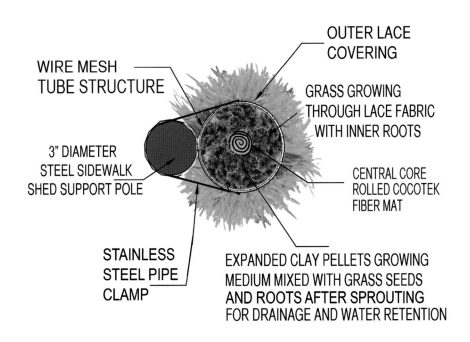

WIRE MESH
TUBE STRUCTURE

OUTER LACE
COVERING

GRASS GROWING
THROUGH LACE FABRIC
WITH INNER ROOTS

3" DIAMETER
STEEL SIDEWALK
SHED SUPPORT POLE

CENTRAL CORE
ROLLED COCOTEK
FIBER MAT

STAINLESS
STEEL PIPE
CLAMP

EXPANDED CLAY PELLETS GROWING
MEDIUM MIXED WITH GRASS SEEDS
AND ROOTS AFTER SPROUTING
FOR DRAINAGE AND WATER RETENTION

Left: Detail of Seed Posts hung from sidewalk shed posts.
Right: Section.

Top: Detail of Seed Posts hung from city fence. Walkway.
Bottom: Entrance area.
Right: View of Seed Posts hung from sidewalk shed posts.

El Charro

Mexico City, Mexico
Ceiling Design: Jeronimo Hagerman
Architectue: Cheremserrano
Completion: 2009
Client: Gastronomica del Amor
Photos: Jaime Navarro, Spain

This Mexican restaurant, located in La Condesa, Mexico, allowed the designers to make an intervention in an existing place, taking care of the functional requirements while satisfying and expressing the client´s character and personality. This project was carried out in collaboration with Mexican artist, Jeronimo Hagerman, who designed the ceiling and called it: "Ando volando bajo" ("I am flying low"). The ceiling is covered by a black, perforated shield. Purple and pink dissected flowers hang in the ceiling creating different forms, which evoke Mexican landscapes of clouds and flowers. The floor is made of dark stone and incorporate a wood platform that takes you into the restaurant.

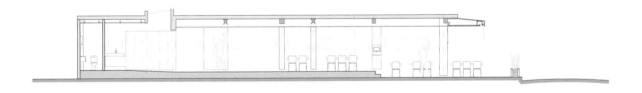

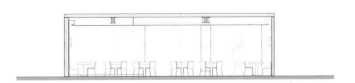

Left: Interior view.
Right: Sections.

Top: View through the restaurant.
Bottom: Perspective.
Right: Ceiling with flowers and large table.

Eco-Boulevard

Madrid, Spain
Landscape Design: ecosistema urbano
Architecture: [ecosistema urbano] architects
Completion: 2007
Client: EMVS – Madrid City Council
Photos: Emilio P. Doiztua

This proposal for the Eco-Boulevard can be defined as an urban recycling project that is comprised of the following steps: the installation of three socially revitalizing 'air tree' areas, the densification of the tree population within its existing location, the reduction of traffic routes, and superficial interventions within the existing urbanization that reconfigure the implemented urban development. The three 'air trees' areas function like open ground sites. Installed as temporary prostheses, they will be used only until airconditioned spaces are no longer needed, and the area becomes 'fixed'. When a sufficient amount of time has passed, these devices shall be dismantled, leaving behind spaces that resemble forest clearings.

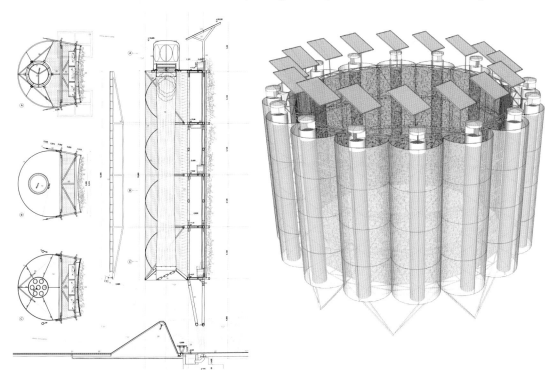

Left: Media Tree, façade.
Right: Climatic tree, section and axonometric.

Top: Media Tree, detail green wall. Climatic Tree, interior.
Bottom: Ludic Tree.
Right: Ludic Tree with Media Tree in the background.

Index

Creatives

Places